The Joy of Friendship

A Celebration of Friendship in Words and Pictures

Robert Scotellaro

Meadowbrook Press

Distributed by Simon & Schuster
New York

Library of Congress has cataloged the original edition as follows:
Scotellaro, Robert.
The joy of friendship / by Robert Scotellaro
    p.   cm.
  1. Friendship—Quotations, maxims,etc.   I. Title
  BF575.F66S38 1996
  177' .6—dc20   96-10963
                                        CIP

ISBN 0-88166-460-X

Simon & Schuster Ordering # 0-684-01913-2

Editor: Bruce Lansky
Editorial Coordinator: David Tobey
Photo Editor: Maggie Merkow
Production Managers: Amy Unger and Paul Woods
Production Coordinator: Danielle White
Cover Design: Peggy Bates
Cover Photography: © Patrick Ramsey/Imagestate

© 2003 by Robert Scotellaro

Published by Meadowbrook Press, 5451 Smetana Drive, Minnetonka, MN 55343
www.meadowbrookpress.com

BOOK TRADE DISTRIBUTION by Simon & Schuster, a division of Simon and Schuster, Inc., 1230 Avenue of the Americas, New York, NY 10020.

08 07 06 05 04 03   10 9 8 7 6 5 4 3 2 1

Printed in the United States of America

Acknowledgments

We would like to thank the individuals who served on a reading panel for this project: Shirley Bingham, Sonja Brown, Chris Bruce, Eileen Daily, Charles Ghigna, Judi James, Jo Kittinger, Sydnie Meltzer Kleinhenz, Barbara Merchant, Robin Michel, Lois Muehl, Claire Puneky, Heidi Roemer, Lawrence Schimel, Denise Tiffany, and Esther Towns.

We would also like to thank the photographers who contributed to this book: pp. 7, 33, and 81 © 1993, 1994, and 1993 respectively by Scott Barrow; pp. 12 and 95 © by Terry Wild; p. 19 © 1996 by Susan Bullard; p. 24 © 1996 by Michael E. Siluk/The Picture Cube; p. 38 © 1990 by Paula Smith; p. 45 © 1977 by Ulrike Welsch; p. 50 © by T. L. Wilmsmeyer; p. 59 © by Rick Lee/SuperStock, Inc.; p. 62 © by Judy Creek; p. 69 © 1996 by Susan Van Etten/The Picture Cube; p. 74 © 1996 by Jim Whitmer; p. 86 © 1990 by Scott Halleran; p. 102 © 1974 by Archie Lieberman, © renewed 1994 by Archie Lieberman.

Dedication

For my mother, Linda Scotellaro,
with love and gratitude

Introduction

Pals, companions, buddies, old friends, and new acquaintances—
to whatever degree they vary, friendships enrich our lives.
Friends are our well-wishers and our advocates. They are our
teammates, our coaches, and our cheerleaders all in one. They
are an extended family that knows no boundaries of age or color
or religion.

Friends challenge us, help us reflect, and put us at ease. They
cry with us and laugh with us. They inspire and heal. And when
life plays rough, they are still there when the dust settles.

In the following pages, I have tried to capture the many facets of
the meaning and value of friends and friendships. When you
share this book with a friend, I hope its words and sentiments
illuminate the true blessing friendship is.

Robert Scotellaro

Friendship is a voyage
you map out
as you go along.

Each friendship is a story that's never before been written.

Friendship is a school of higher education where the doors are always open.

Sometimes a friend is a mirror,
sometimes a window looking out
into a bigger world.

Sometimes friendship
is the wind in our sails.
Sometimes it is calm waters.

Friends are the "family members"
you actually get to choose.

Friends are more interested in
who you are than
who you are expected to be.

Friendship is sharing
a common bond
that doesn't bind.

When life is a desert,
friendship is a cool glass of water.

Having a friend is not a means to an end
but an end in itself.

Friendship is strong medicine.

Children may be little,
but their friendships are not.

A friend is a person who goes around
talking behind your back—
saying nice things!

Friendship is not having to act bubbly when
you're feeling flat.

When assessing your wealth,
don't look to your bankbook—
look to your friends.

Friendships pay better dividends
than any bank.

You never question the cost of friendship
once you understand its value.

The glue that holds friendships together
cannot be purchased at any price.

When a friend gives a present, it is not the
present, but the friend that is the gift.

Sharing a good dream makes it more so—
sharing a bad dream makes it less so.

Friends share good and bad
without keeping score.

Sharing a piece of bread
with a friend
can be a feast.

Nothing beats sharing a new idea
with an old friend.

Friends share not only cups of laughter,
but also cups of sorrow.

Sharing worries can make them disappear.

Shared sorrows lend sweetness to the
shared joys that follow.

Friends are willing to share
not only what they have,
but also what they are.

A child who shares her last cookie with a
friend shares a great love.

The plastic ring a small child gives a friend
is worth a million bucks.

The fountain of youth is found
in the laughter of friends.

Friends laugh with each other,
not at each other.

The tears of friends, very often,
are from laughter.

Friends may compete hard against each other on the playing field and still have a good time together off it.

Sometimes it's important for friends
just to be silly together.

Friends can be silly together
without feeling silly about it.

What a wonderful sight:
two young friends playing in
a cardboard box, just back from
a voyage in outer space.

Life is short. Enjoy your friends.

Invent your own holiday, and send
a friend a card in celebration.

Sometimes all you need is a movie,
a friend, and a big bowl of popcorn.

Working with a friend
turns work into fun.

Friends forgive you for the
surprise birthday parties
you spring on them.

Planning a trip with a friend
can be nearly as enjoyable
as the trip itself.

Sitting in front of a fireplace,
sharing dreams with a friend,
can turn an old rug into a flying carpet.

When you lose the pulse
of a particular dream,
a friend can help you
put your finger back on it.

Good friends affirm each other's dreams.

Friends not only share history,
but also make history.

Friends stop to smell the roses,
then take time to plant a few.

Sometimes it takes a friend
to point out the treasures
right under our noses.

Friends take time to discover
the best in each other.

Friends can see the best in each other,
even when they're at their worst.

Don't let a friend put you on a pedestal
unless there's room enough
for both of you.

Ordinary friends find each other
extraordinary.

Friends allow you to be not only yourself
but also the self you want to be.

Friends delight in each other's
self-discovery.

Friends are quick to point out
opportunities for each other.

Friends can solve
the world's problems
over a cup of coffee.

Friends take turns holding the ladder
for each other to climb.

Between friends, vulnerability
is strength, not weakness.

Those who say they have
more friends than they can count
are including the ones
they can't count on.

Trust is what makes
a friend's advice so valuable.

Trust is the coin
of the realm of friendship.

What is more eloquent
than the comfortable silence
between friends?

The only etiquette required
for a friend is "Be yourself."

Being yourself when you're not
feeling like yourself is something
you can do around friends.

What matters to a friend
matters to you.

Good friends know when to be invisible.

Good friends know your moods,
and respect them.

Friends don't have to spell
everything out for each other.

The benefit that close friends have,
when meeting for a chat,
is they don't need to effervesce,
when they are feeling flat.

Friends don't need to declare their bond.
It is stated most eloquently
through their actions.

Two buddies screeching
like a couple of alley cats
to the tune of a favorite song
is the sweetest music of all.

The harmony between friends
is sweeter than any choir.

It's wonderful when a family member
is also a friend.

The touch of a good friend
can be healing.

Sometimes a library of words
cannot say what a hug can.

There's enough warmth in a friend's hug
to warm up the coldest day.

Family members know
the child you have been;
friends know the adult
you have become.

The bond between
a student and a teacher
can forge a strong friendship.

The most important
friend you make is yourself.
Then all others can follow.

To have a friend, be a friend.

First you must be a whole person
before you can be half of a relationship.

It is easier to accept a friend's faults
once you have acknowledged your own.

The pace of friendship is a stroll,
not a race.

There are no blueprints for friendships.
Each one is custom-made.

Acceptance is the fruit of friendship.

Intimacy cannot be hurried.

People evolve,
and the friendships that endure
evolve right along with them.

Good friends use the past,
not for a house, but for a foundation.

It takes work and play
to keep a friendship going.

Friendships need to be flexible
as well as strong.

The ability to stretch and bend is what
gives a friendship durability.

Sometimes it is better
to look over,
and sometimes it is better
to overlook.

Pettiness should be avoided
between friends—
people stumble over pebbles,
never mountains.

Friends don't have to be the same;
they just have to share
the same commitment.

Often the very young and the very old make the best of friends.

Friends must value each other's privacy
as much as their togetherness.

It's not important to agree
with every conviction a friend might have.
But it is important to respect them.

Sometimes it is our differences,
rather than our similarities,
that keep our friendships growing.

It is important for friends to celebrate
the uniqueness they see in each other.

What a great pleasure it is
to see the children of friends
become friends!

It's great when your new friend
and old friend hit it off.

When friends discuss their worries,
they make molehills out of mountains.

A warm conversation with a friend
can take the chill out of a cool day.

Sometimes friends must cry together
before they can laugh together.

When we are looking for answers,
sometimes a friend can supply
the right questions.

No one can read between the lines
better than a close friend.

Sometimes friends need to hear
your words and sometimes
just their own, while you listen.

Sometimes it's important for friends
to listen with their hearts,
and not just their heads.

A history of friendship
is not enough to sustain it.
You need to stay in touch.

Miles may lie between them,
but friends remain connected.

Sometimes having an open mind
means keeping a closed mouth.

A friend is someone with whom
you can think out loud.

It is often more important to be heard
than to be analyzed.

To be a friend, it helps to bend.

The friend who forgives is easiest to forgive.

Give and *take* are the twin pillars
of friendship.

A friend will meet you halfway,
even when halfway is a long way off.

Friendship requires compromise
without feeling compromised.

Friends give their best and the best
comes back to them.

The distances we travel over hard times
are shortened when a friend is with us.

The darkest moments can be brightened
by the light in a friend's eyes.

Friends can help provide safe passage
through troubled waters.

Sometimes crisis can
create friendships.

Adversity has a way of
reintroducing friends to each other.

Nothing strengthens the roots
of friendship like shared adversity.

True friendships endure the worst of times.

"For richer and for poorer,
in sickness and in health"
works for friendships, too.

Friendships weather all seasons.

Tough times can fashion a friendship
as strong as steel.

When you're not feeling well,
a visit from a friend is good medicine.

A friend brings not only a plant and a card
when visiting you in the hospital,
but comfort and concern as well.

A friend can make you laugh
when you're not feeling well.

When you've painted yourself
into a corner,
it sometimes takes a friend
to remind you that the paint will dry.

Fair-weather friends are never in season.

Lifting up a friend's spirits
can be uplifting.

Friends take the pain
out of life's ups and downs.

It is hard to defeat hope
when two hopes are joined.

A friend can add clarity
when you're all mixed up:

When you're beating yourself up
about something,
a friend can soften the blows.

When friends lose their way,
it's important to offer a hand,
and not a wagging finger.

Friends are magicians—they can make
each other's worries disappear.

When safety systems snap and fail us,
when bumps along the line derail us,
it's good to know
friends have the knack
to help each other back on track.

When trouble shows its face,
a good friend shows her face, too.

When the odds are against you,
friends help even the score.

Friends help us catch up
when we have had a setback.

Sometimes a friend can tell you
what you can't even tell yourself.

We often tell friends what's wrong.
They often point out to us what's right.

Sometimes a friend's frankness
can be the deepest expression of caring.

Sometimes we ask too much
of those we care about
and sometimes not enough.

If you want a friend who's never
critical—get a dog!

Friends care enough to take the risk,
to tell you loud and clear,
the things you really know are true,
but might not want to hear.

There's no more welcomed sound
than a friend's sound advice.

With friends, the roles of teacher and student
may change several times
in a single conversation.

Friends help each other
learn from their mistakes.

"Help!" can be whispered softly,
and a friend will hear it.

When everyone else has an excuse,
friends don't hesitate to help.

When it comes to helping,
friends have no problem
with on-the-job training.

Friends can accept help
as easily as they offer it.

Friends take turns
shoring up each other's weaknesses
and applauding each other's strengths.

An enemy will take advantage
of your mistakes—
a friend will help you correct them.

Sometimes friends are on
the playing field with you,
and sometimes on the sidelines
cheering you on.

Sometimes it takes a push
to get a friend going.
Sometimes it takes a hug.

A friend can help you accomplish
what you didn't even know
you could accomplish.

Friends not only help you look for
the light at the end of the tunnel—
they bring a flashlight!

Friends cannot suffer each other's wounds,
but they can help in the healing process.

Friends help each other
turn the errors of the past
into future successes.

It is important not only to know you love,
but to show you love.

The best way a friend can teach
is by example.

Friends allow each other
to make mistakes.

Friends keep an eye out
for your blind side.

Friends help each other accept
when acceptance is needed
and change when change is needed.

True friends are not just there for the feast,
but for the famine as well.

One friend beside you
when the chips are down is worth
a thousand toasting your prosperity.

Friends are the ones who are still there
after the dust settles.

A friend will believe in you
even when you don't believe in yourself.

Friends are there to remind each other
that often failure is the first step to success.

Knowing a friend is nearby
can make a timid spirit brave.

When you count your friends,
you're counting your blessings.

Friends can't provide the wings
if you want to fly.
But it's nice to know
they'll be there with a safety net.

The best gift a friend can give
is his presence.

Sometimes friends
make the best therapists,
and they don't charge by the hour.

Some of the greatest riches
are stored in photo albums.

Looking through a shoe box
for a photo of an old friend
is like digging for buried treasure.

Our memories make
the greatest picture albums.

Reminiscing makes old friends
young again.

A friend's happy memories
are often yours, too.

Good memories
are a renewable resource.

It's great running into a friend
after many years
and finding the warmth still there.

Sometimes a long break in a friendship
can be bridged in a matter of seconds
by a hug.

It's a pleasure when
two retired friends finally have time
for long visits with each other.

Good friends can really go back—
and also forward.

What a joy it is to travel a new road
with an old friend.

You may read your closest friend
from cover to cover a thousand times
and still find a chapter you've missed.

Time isn't spent with a friend—
it's invested.

Old friends can still surprise each other
with new insights.

The harvests friends reap
are from seeds planted long ago.

The years fade away
when old friends get together.

The Joy of Marriage

by Monica and Bill Dodds

Here's a book of romance and love for married couples. With clever one-line messages, it accentuates the everyday romantic, caring, and playful elements of married life:

- A marriage license is really just a learner's permit.
- Love is letting your spouse have the last piece of pie.
- The great thing about being married a long time is falling in love with the same person again...and again...and again.

Filled with beautiful, touching black-and-white photographs, it's the perfect gift for weddings and anniversaries.

Order #3504

The Joy of Parenthood

by Jan Blaustone

This book contains hundreds of warm and inspirational "nuggets" of wisdom to help prepare parents for the pleasures and challenges ahead. Twenty-four touching black-and-white photos help convey the joy of parenthood and make this a delightful book to give or receive.

Order #3500

Familiarity Breeds Children
selected by Bruce Lansky

Lansky has created a humor book for parents that will delight and revive them. This collection is a treasury of the most outrageous and clever things ever said about raising children by world-class comedians and humorists including Roseanne, Erma Bombeck, Bill Cosby, Dave Barry, Mark Twain, Fran Lebowitz, and others. Filled with entertaining photographs, it makes the perfect gift for any parents you know—including yourself. Originally entitled *The Funny Side of Parenthood*.

Order #4015

The Joy of Grandparenting
by Audrey Sherins
and Joan Holleman

This book will have grandparents smiling in agreement as they read these modern proverbs. It contains wit and wisdom on such issues as grandparents as models; passing on family heritage; the uniqueness of each grandchild; the role of grandparent, parent, and child; showing off grandchildren; and the future. Audrey Sherins describes being a grandparent as "all the pleasure and none of the responsibility of parenthood."

Order #3502

Order Form

Qty.	Title	Author	Order No.	Unit Cost	Total
	Age Happens	Lansky, B.	4025	$7.00	
	Are You Over the Hill?	Dodds, B.	4265	$6.00	
	Baby Name Personality Survey	Lansky/Sinrod	1270	$7.00	
	Best Baby Shower Book	Cooke, C.	1239	$7.00	
	Best Party Book	Warner, P.	6089	$7.00	
	Best Wedding Shower	Cooke, C.	6059	$7.00	
	Dads Say the Dumbest Things!	Lansky/Jones	4220	$6.00	
	Familiarity Breeds Children	Lansky, B.	4015	$7.00	
	For Better and For Worse	Lansky, B.	4000	$7.00	
	Golf: It's Just a Game	Lansky, B.	4035	$7.00	
	Grandma Knows Best	McBride, M.	4009	$6.00	
	Joy of Friendship	Scotellaro, R.	3506	$7.00	
	Joy of Grandparenting	Sherins/Holleman	3502	$7.00	
	Joy of Marriage	Dodds, M. & B.	3504	$7.00	
	Joy of Parenthood	Blaustone, J.	3500	$6.00	
	Maternal Journal	Bennett, M.	3171	$10.00	
	Moms Say the Funniest Things!	Lansky, B.	4280	$6.00	
				Subtotal	
			Shipping and Handling (see below)		
			MN residents add 6.5% sales tax		
				Total	

YES! Please send me the books indicated above. Add $2.00 shipping and handling for the first book and 50¢ for each additional book. Add $2.50 to total for books shipped to Canada. Overseas postage will be billed. Allow up to four weeks for delivery. Send check or money order payable to Meadowbrook Press. No cash or COD's, please. Prices subject to change without notice. Quantity discounts available upon request.

Send book(s) to:

Name _____ Address _____

City _____ State ____ Zip _____ Telephone (____) _____

P.O. number (if necessary) _____ Payment via: ❑ Check or money order payable to Meadowbrook Press

Amount enclosed $ _____ ❑ Visa ❑ MasterCard (for orders over $10.00 only)

Account # _____ Signature _____ Exp. Date _____

A *FREE* Meadowbrook Press catalog is available upon request.

Mail to:
Meadowbrook, Inc.
18318 Minnetonka Boulevard, Deephaven, MN 55391

(612) 473-5400   Toll-Free 1-800-338-2232   Fax (612) 475-0736